UNSHAKABLE

UNSHAKABLE

WRITTEN BY

Joan McLeod

MARIGOLD PRESS BOOKS

A division of International School of Story

Copyright © 2024 JOAN MCLEOD

All rights reserved. No portion of this book may be reproduced, stored in a retrieval system, or transmitted in any form or by any means–electronic, mechanical, photocopy, recording, scanning, or other–except for brief quotations in critical reviews or articles, without the prior written permission of the author.

Published in Savannah, Georgia by Marigold Press Books, a division of International School of Story.

Marigold Press Books titles may be purchased in bulk for educational, business, fund-raising, or sales promotional use. For information, please email marigoldpressbooks@gmail.com.

Fonts and stock images licensed for commercial use. AI used to generate cover art.

Author: McLeod, Joan
Title: Unshakable
ISBN: 978-1-942923-79-4
Library of Congress Control Number: xxxxxxxxx
Cover Design: Rebekah McLeod

ACKNOWLEDGEMENTS

I thank Almighty God whose hand has always been on my life.

To the women religious of the Ursuline Convent, Barbados, who laid the spiritual foundation from which I draw strength during life's most challenging times.

To my five loving children who taught me how to find ways to balance my obligations. Cliphane ll, Lucien, Travis, and Nicel my twins, and Natacha, you kept me going when life was toughest. Thank you!

To my twin granddaughters Layla and Millay who bring much love and joy to my life.

To Rebekah and Emra without whose encouragement this story might have remained untold. I offer my humble and sincerest thanks.

TABLE OF CONTENTS

The Beginning 1
Back to Our Roots 5
A New Chapter 11
The Crossroads of Sacred Service 17
Aspirations, Resolve, and Education 23
Serving in the Armed Forces 29
Flight Nurse Wings 35
The Beginning of Married Life 39
The Family Grows 47
Georgia Living 53
The Children 57
Team Spirit 89, Off to War 61
Parents move to Georgia 71
An Unforgettable Birthday 77
Retirement 85
The Unraveling 93
A New Beginning 107
About the Author 115

UNSHAKABLE

TO THE READER

It is my hope that among these pages, you, the reader, will find encouragement to:

Ask God or your higher power to guide you through life's rough patches;

Move past any pain you may experience;

Find the things in life that give you a sense of fulfillment;

To learn to not depend solely on your partner to make you happy;

To find ways to improve the lives of others if even in small ways.

THE BEGINNING

In the radiant embrace of the summer of 1946, I made my debut into a world buzzing with the echoes of a post-war era. Born into the union of two souls rooted in the sun-kissed soil of the Caribbean Island of Barbados, my existence carried the rhythmic cadence of tropical winds and the warmth of golden sands.

My mother, a flower transplanted across the vast Atlantic to New York, was brought to the shores of the United States under the guidance of her paternal aunt. With her came the vibrance of Bajan traditions, intertwined with the fabric of her new American surroundings. It was here she met my father—a man whose roots, like hers, burrowed deep into the rich Barbadian earth, yet he was born in the USA as his parents moved to the USA and made their life here. United by the shared history of an island paradise, they forged a new chapter in their new evolving world.

Together, they navigated the challenges of adapting to a new land while preserving the essence of their island roots. I, the firstborn, became the bridge between the two worlds, the fusion of the Barbadian spirit and American dreams.

In my earliest recollections, scattered images swirl like fragments of a forgotten dream. One vignette, however, stands out among the rest, etched in the corridors of my mind with a peculiar blend of innocence and sorrow.

I remember the teacup, a fragile vessel perched on a shelf like a relic of grown-up rituals. The allure of curiosity overcame me, prompting the mischievous act of snatching it from its place and letting it plummet to the floor, the symphony of shattering porcelain accompanied by my mother's swift intervention—a stern "NO" that served as one of my first lessons in boundaries.

Yet, it was another memory that lingered, haunting the corners of my consciousness. It was an evening wrapped in an unfamiliar stillness, as a male cousin, an occasional visitor in our quiet home, tucked me into a makeshift bed on the living room sofa. Questions flitted through my young mind like fireflies in the dark—*why this deviation from the routine, and where was my mother?*

Beyond the walls of our modest apartment, voices ebbed and flowed, a cacophony of hushed conversations that only intensified my sense of disquiet. The absence of my mother fueled my curiosity, as I strained to grasp the echoes of her whereabouts. The last image I held was of her departing to hang laundry on the roof—an ordinary chore that would soon transform into a poignant memory.

Years later, the narrative unfolded with a painful clarity. The rooftop, once a mundane setting for household tasks, became the stage for a tragedy that altered the course of my family's history. At the tender age of three, my innocence shielded me from the gravity of the event. I learned, and could not fathom, that my mother had chosen to jump off the rooftop of the building and end her own life.

A cruel revelation pierced through the shroud of time: my father's betrayal, an extramarital affair, and the impending arrival of a half-sibling had become the harbingers of my mother's despair. In a heart-wrenching decision, she opted to step into the abyss, leaving behind a shattered family—me and my eleven-month-old sister. Leaving us with the unraveling threads of a once-whole love story.

The indelible scars of that tumultuous chapter linger, woven into the fabric of my existence. Each teacup clang, every rustle of bed sheets on that living room sofa, served as a whispered echo of a life forever altered by a mother's silent struggles.

BACK TO OUR ROOTS

My father was a Merchant Marine and his prolonged absences, lasting months at a time, posed a conundrum for our care. None among our kinfolk seemed willing to shoulder the responsibility of caring for both me and my sister simultaneously. In this familial quandary, it was my maternal grandmother who extended a heartfelt offer to ease the burden.

She conveyed a poignant message to my father, "Bring the girls to me," proposing a solution that would keep our sibling unity intact by bringing us to Barbados, where she pledged to nurture and protect us under her watchful gaze. I, as a six-year-old, found myself aboard an airplane for the first time, the anticipation tinged with the excitement of a new adventure. I still recall the green plaid dress with the white trim bodice I wore for that momentous journey, a vivid snapshot in the album of my early memories.

As we alighted on the shores of Barbados, my grandmother welcomed us with open arms, "Look at little Beattie," she said as she hugged me tightly. My mom's name was Beatrice, Beattie, her nickname. Granny's joy was palpable at having her daughter's offspring under her care. Grandma was only five foot four, small in stature, with beautiful brown eyes. With fatherly love and a heavy heart, my dad entrusted us to her care before returning to the United States, bridging the geographical gap with the promise of reunions to come.

Our entry into Barbadian life included enrollment in a Catholic school, a cornerstone of our education in this newfound chapter. To ensure our safe passage to and from school, our grandmother's youngest sister became our daily companion on the bus rides. These elementary school days unfolded in a seemingly ordinary fashion, yet they held a ritual that would shape the foundation of my spiritual journey.

Each day, after the noonday meal, the echoes of collective prayer resonated through the chapel—the recitation of the Rosary. The Rosary consists of five decades, the "Our Father who art in Heaven, hallowed be Thy Name, Thy kingdom come, Thy will be done on earth as it is in heaven." This is followed by ten Hail Marys. Hail Mary is a prayer, a sentence of it being, "Hail Mary full of grace, the Lord is with thee, blessed art thou among women, and blessed is the fruit of thy womb, Jesus." Then we say, "Glory be to the Father, and to the Son, and to the Holy Spirit, as it was in the beginning, is now, and ever shall be, world without end, Amen."

This practice, lasting about half an hour, marked the genesis of my faith formation. Despite the passage of time, communal prayers became a cherished routine, a shared expression of spirituality that united the students in a quiet symphony of devotion, making the time seemingly slip away in our collective faith.

Basking in the island's perpetual embrace, my childhood unfolded with warmth and joy. Throughout the year, my maternal grandfather emerged as a figure of enchantment, an unconventional fisherman whose methods defied the norm.

Devoid of a boat, yet possessing an uncanny prowess, my grandfather would venture to the beach and return with an abundance of seafood that could sustain us for days. Under his guidance, I discovered the artistry of capturing small fish with a net and the exhilarating skill of spearing diverse species using an iron rod. Those sun-drenched summertime days, free from the confines of school, became a world of maritime adventures. Hours spent at the beach transformed into a treasure hunt, and I'd return home triumphant, a proud collector of the ocean's bounty.

In my grandmother's vibrant neighborhood, a chorus of laughter and playful footsteps echoed through the air, for it was a haven for many children. As young voyagers from America, we found ourselves elevated to a status akin to celebrities. The neighbors, familiar with my mother's own childhood escapades, welcomed us with open arms. Their eyes lit up with nostalgia, seemingly delighted to witness the next generation of our family making the island their home.

Our humble abode stood as the unofficial headquarters for neighborhood kids seeking refuge after the final school bell chimed and on weekends teeming with laughter and play. Here in the streets, where the absence of running water and electricity was a shared reality, our home emerged as a beacon of camaraderie.

At the street's end, a communal standpipe became the daily pilgrimage site for our neighbors, a place where jerry cans were filled with the water that sustained our households. It was a life of survival, where my grandmother, the matriarch of our domain, spared no effort. She enlisted the help of someone to fetch our daily water supply, a precious liquid that trickled into the heart of our home.

As the sun dipped below the horizon, our evenings unfolded in the soft glow of kerosene lamps. In the absence of electricity, these lamps became the custodians of our nocturnal adventures, casting flickering shadows that danced upon the walls and illuminated the shared spaces where stories were exchanged, and bonds were forged. Being an avid reader, I always had to be encouraged to go to bed. Grandma would always say, "Joan, it's time to put the light out and get ready for bed." Reluctantly, I'd put away my book, brush my teeth, wash my face, and go to bed.

The rhythm of sustenance in our home echoed the resilience of my grandmother's hands. Beyond the threshold, a patchwork of fruits and vegetables thrived under her nurturing touch, transforming the backyard into a micro-farm including chickens, ducks, and turkeys. For a fleeting period, sheep, goats, and pigs added their voices to the lively symphony, enriching our lives with the ebb and flow of rural existence. It was an oasis of simplicity, a haven where the essentials of life were shared, where the laughter of children echoed in harmony with the animals.

In my teenage years, some weekends bore witness to a unique responsibility— ferrying eggs and freshly slaughtered chickens to white families who held a deep appreciation for the bounty cultivated by Granny's skilled hands. My grandmother wasn't just a cultivator of the land; her hands crafted cakes that transcended mere confections—they were edible canvases, masterpieces adorned with meticulous decorations destined for weddings and joyous gatherings.

In this bustling theater of our kitchen, I found a front-row seat to the enchanting process. Mesmerized, I would perch beside Granny, my eyes fixed on her nimble fingers as they deftly placed each decoration with an artist's precision. Hours would slip away unnoticed, and I'd linger, eager to witness the transformation of raw ingredients into a culinary work of art.

A NEW CHAPTER

As the summer came to its end, I embarked on my journey into Secondary school, and a new chapter unfolded. Propelled by commendable grades, I found myself on the path to the Ursuline Convent—a private Catholic school that beckoned with promises of knowledge and camaraderie. This institution, nestled in tradition, stood primarily as a boarding school, welcoming students not only from my island but from distant shores, forming a mosaic of cultural diversity.

In this setting, my adolescence unfolded, filled with responsibilities, family traditions, and the promise of education in the company of kindred spirits. I loved being a day student at the Ursuline Convent. The convent was a large compound with several buildings, one building for Montessori up to third grade, one for the freshman, and the boarding school dorms with some classes. The main building housed the nuns, the school library, and the accounting hall. A grassy knoll that led to the auditorium lay in between the building and the swimming pool. Behind the Chapel and adjacent to this were the fields for track, netball, and softball. The campus was beautiful, with many flowering trees, and a little grotto with a statue of our Lady.

Within the halls of the Ursuline Convent, I discovered a microcosm of interconnected worlds, where voices from various islands and countries melded into a chorus of shared experiences. The majority of my classmates hailed from Venezuela, weaving the vibrant threads of South American culture into our academic pursuits.

I learned the common greeting and reply as we started our days together. We didn't have much interaction during lunch breaks as they were boarders and ate lunch separately from us, and I scurried home after class to do homework and deliver an evening meal to a friend of my grandmother's. Yet we had a few celebratory days when they dressed up in their colorful skirts and blouses and shared their lovely songs and dances.

Even though I didn't meet with my peers who were fluent in Spanish often outside of the classroom, I eagerly embraced the challenge of learning the language to connect with them, sparking a passion that would endure beyond the classroom walls and accompany me through my college years. Fortunately, we had to take Spanish classes at school and being surrounded by my Spanish peers helped so much!

The Ursuline sisters cultivated not only academic excellence but also a profound sense of service and community. Our curriculum extended beyond textbooks, delving into electives like cooking and sewing, enriching our education with practical life skills. Physical well-being became a focal point, and our school proudly claimed the distinction of being the island's first and only institution with a swimming pool—a testament to our commitment to holistic development.

High school, for me, became a realm of joyous competition, where our annual sports meets were anticipated with eager enthusiasm. The thrill of the track, the camaraderie of teammates, and the shared pursuit of excellence painted those years with vibrant hues of youthful exuberance.

As I stood on the precipice of post-secondary endeavors, an unexpected opportunity was presented to me. The Headmistress of the public Catholic school, recognizing my dedication to service encapsulated in our school motto, Serviam (I will serve), asked me to assist in teaching a special education class. Embarking on this venture, I faced a diverse range of students, from the youngest at seven to a pair of sixteen-year-old boys with little formal schooling from other islands.

Crafting lessons that engaged every student presented its challenges, but witnessing the pride gleaming in their eyes upon mastering a lesson became the most fulfilling reward. For a full semester, I devoted myself to this endeavor, sowing the seeds of knowledge and resilience.

As the chapter concluded, it became apparent that I would bid the island farewell, to return to the United States of America.

My Godmother frequently visited Barbados and when she visited in the spring, knowing I was about to finish high school, she felt I needed to go back to the United States. She spoke to my father, who was at sea, and they decided I should go and live with my aunt and uncle in Brooklyn, New York.

Granny had promised my dad she would take care of us and provide us with an education, but she knew it was time for me to go, as Barbados couldn't give me what the United States would. We were both very tearful, and I held onto the knowledge that I would always carry with me the indelible imprints of this transformative high school journey—a journey not only of personal growth but one marked by the spirit of service and the joy of empowering others through education.

THE CROSSROADS OF SACRED SERVICE

Upon my return to the States, with my father overseas, the decision was made that I would reside with my aunt and her husband. They lived in the upper echelons of a brownstone nestled in the heart of Brooklyn. In this familial haven, a multi-story sanctuary of shared spaces and intertwined lives, my uncle—my father's youngest brother—occupied the ground floor with his own family, comprising of his wife and two sons, a preschooler, and a second grader.

In this peaceful home, the boys, with their well-mannered demeanor, tiptoed through the house like silent sprites, leaving me almost oblivious to their presence. Yet, on weekends, I would seize the opportunity to part the curtain of domestic routine, guiding the young duo to the park that sprawled enticingly across the street. There, amidst the laughter echoing off playground equipment, our bonds grew stronger.

During moments when their mother needed to embark on errands, I gladly assumed the role of caretaker, relishing the chance to be enveloped in the growing infectious energy of my younger cousins. As I watched over them and shared laughter and imaginative games, the occasional adventure unfolded. The boys loved me to spin around with them, and on one of these days, the eldest boy let go of my hand and fell onto the coffee table. He hit the side of his face and ended up with a goose egg above his eye. I felt awful, quickly icing his eye, and when his mom returned she said, "Boys will be boys," being more concerned about my feelings. It did leave me quite nervous in the days ahead, but thankful that was the worst outcome of our escapades.

Nestled within the vibrance of Brooklyn, our neighborhood painted a rich portrait of diversity, a melting pot of Italian, Hispanic, Jewish, and African American residents. We lived on a street lined with trees and walking down the block one could hear several different languages. Everyone was cordial with one another, exchanging greetings. The homeowners took pride in their surroundings and who they were. Frequently you would see the women sweeping their courtyards enjoying the quiet. Once the children were outside on their breaks, chatter and laughter filled the air.

At the end of our street stood a Catholic elementary school, its architectural sturdiness echoed by a church opposite, both serving as pillars of spiritual and educational guidance. It was here that I found myself drawn to the ritual of daily Mass. The church's Greystone facade illuminated by sunlight streaming through stained glass windows created a sacred ambiance that transcended the ordinary.

My educational journey unfolded within the hallowed walls of the Catholic school, which taught students spanning from elementary to high school. The religious women who graced the classrooms with their wisdom became not just instructors but beacons of influence, shaping my character with the values of service, kindness, and compassion. Under their guidance, the practice of daily prayer became more than a routine—it became a sacred dialogue with the Divine.

Inspired by these holy women, their devotion, and their unwavering commitment to others, I felt a calling to emulate their path. The idea of becoming a sister took root within me, a seed of purpose nurtured by the values instilled during my formative years. Eager to explore this aspiration, I shared my desire with my guardians, who, understanding the gravity of my decision, facilitated a discussion with one of the priests from our cherished church.

In the intimate setting of our home, the priest became a guide in navigating the many ambitions I had. The priest first asked me, "Why do you want to become a sister?" I told him it was something I felt I should do because of my interaction with the Ursuline Sisters. "You know this is a life-long commitment," he went on to remind me. "I know this," I answered. "There is a cost, you will need to provide a dowry for your livelihood," he said. I didn't ask how much this would be as I was so sensitive about money matters. We thanked him for the information and he left.

Uncle George asked me if I knew about the financial implications. I told him I did not and would never expect them to provide this for me and would think about this. As this weighty revelation of the dowry for my room and board at the convent unfolded, the idea of burdening my already supportive relatives with such a financial commitment was inconceivable. Aware of my dependency on them for my current living arrangements, I couldn't fathom imposing additional financial strains on them.

With the determination to carve out an alternative path, I started researching how I could study, work, and become financially self-sufficient. The blueprint included finding employment, enrolling in the local community college, and seeking divine guidance for a career that aligned with my aspirations. In heartfelt discussions with my guardians, we explored the possibilities. Uncle George said with my proficiency in math and science, coupled with the financial constraints ruling out medical school, I should consider the realm of pharmacy. Resolute to shoulder the responsibility one semester at a time, I sought out a course that intertwined pragmatism with passion.

ASPIRATIONS, RESOLVE, AND EDUCATION

The 1960s presented a unique challenge. In the absence of a formal high school graduation ceremony at the convent in Barbados, I needed to pass the GED – a prerequisite for college acceptance. Undeterred, I embraced the task. The GED became not just an academic milestone but a bridge to my aspirations waiting to be realized.

Embracing the challenge of pursuing education after conquering the GED exam, I stepped into the world of academia while juggling a demanding work life. I secured a position as a receptionist at a real estate company, and then began the dual journey, adding my studies at the New York City Community College.

Amid the hustle of work and studies, I delved into a diverse array of courses, from Physics and

Chemistry to Spanish Literature. Buoyed by commendable grades, a year later I made the leap to St John's University, where Pharmacy became my chosen major. The transition necessitated a change in my daily rhythm, needing a revised work schedule to accommodate the demands of full-time academic pursuits.

I took a job at a bank, processing and encoding checks from 11 pm to 7 am. Mornings were a blur of activity, with a modest breakfast preceding a subway ride to class. After my classes, I would rush back home, eat a quick meal, and surrender to sleep to prepare for the night ahead. The arduous schedule tested my resilience, with moments in class occasionally accompanied by involuntary nods.

One night during my work shift while I was busy processing checks, one of my coworkers came over to my workstation and told me that one of his male friends wanted to meet me. I was a conscientious worker interested in production—not socializing—during work hours. My response was, "You can bring your friend over to my workstation and introduce him to me."

Shortly afterward he brought this six-foot-tall, handsome young man with hazel eyes over to meet me.

"Hello, I'm Cliphane, known as Cliff because everyone tends to mispronounce my name." I acknowledged him and kept on working. I later learned that the guys in his section told him not to waste his time trying to talk to me and that he would not even get to first base because I was a no-nonsense girl whose only interest was my education.

A few days after the introduction I found out that some of my co-workers who lived in Brooklyn carpooled with my new acquaintance after work. I was asked to join them. Cliff asked me to sit in the front seat between him and his friend who introduced us. At one point during the ride home, he made a hard turn which caused me to lean on him. This was the beginning of five years of courtship and fifty years of marriage. It was a slow-building relationship as I was so focused on my studies and working many hours.

One morning, after the lecture curtain had fallen, a concerned professor asked me to stay behind. He expressed his apprehensions about my ability to focus in class. "I see you nodding off during my lectures. Are you getting enough rest?" When I told him that I work at night, he replied that to pass would require my undivided attention. I told him the reality of having a job was an essential component enabling my attendance at St John's.

I put in extra hours for his class, as I had to pass it while still keeping my job. I did pass the class and then opted for a lighter credit load in the subsequent semester. My determination to succeed and attain my goals pressed me to somehow find a way to make everything work.

Amidst the many academic choices, a realization dawned on me—I could lighten my load by tackling a summer course. I chose organic chemistry, a decision that brought unforeseen challenges. As the class commenced, the stark truth emerged—my prior chemistry courses at New York City Community College had left me ill-prepared for the rigors of St John's.

I persevered for a few days, grappling with the demanding material. I had to admit that maintaining satisfactory grades was an uphill battle. Acknowledging the need for a recalibration, I made the bold decision to drop the course and, in a swift turn, changed my major to psychology. I realized I had a deep desire to help others and was delighted with this new focus.

For two years, I explored this world of psychology at St John's and then found myself at a crossroads once again. As the foundational psychology courses loomed ahead, an inexplicable nudge directed me away from the path I had initially chosen. The exact moment of this revelation eludes my memory, but the calling became clear—I wanted to become a nurse. Faced with rejection from Hunter College due to my high school grades, I ventured into the unknown, delving into researching the places that offered nursing. I discovered to my surprise that Cornell University's medical and nursing schools were affiliated with the New York Hospital in Manhattan.

Empowered by faith and the conviction that, "In all things God works for the good of those who love Him" (Romans 8:28), I boldly submitted my application to Cornell. With the ink on the envelope still fresh, I went to Puerto Rico to visit my father, who was living there with his third wife. During the visit, all I could think of was this bold choice I had made to pursue nursing. Somehow I knew I was made for it. My path up to that point had been shaped by resilience, faith, and an unwavering belief in the transformative power of unforeseen turns.

Returning from Puerto Rico, a letter awaited me—an invitation to interview with the admissions office at Cornell University-New York Hospital School of Nursing. Seizing the opportunity, I faced the panel with anticipation and determination. Following the interview, a crucial inquiry surfaced—had I applied elsewhere?

Admitting that the interpretation of my high school grades posed a challenge, I found an unexpected ally in Mrs DeWerth, a guiding force within the admissions process. She proposed an audacious solution: "Reach out to the Dean at Hunter College School of Nursing to explain the nuances of the British grading system." I couldn't do this, I simply didn't know if this would impact the outcome positively. I paused.

Days later, a letter of acceptance to Cornell arrived. Not only that but also a substantial scholarship, something I never deemed possible! God's providence, woven into the fabric of my journey, had swung open the doors to Cornell University, an institution that seemed beyond the realm of my wildest dreams.

Having completed the prerequisites for nursing school, I studied fiercely, earning my Bachelor of Science degree in a swift two and a half years. The symbiotic relationship between learning and practical experience manifested as I transitioned from student nurse to graduate nurse. I began working as a Licensed Practical Nurse at the very hospital where my scholarship journey began while I awaited taking the licensing exam to become a Registered Nurse.

SERVING IN THE ARMED FORCES

Driven by a philosophy of service, I decided to enlist in the armed forces, not only to fulfill my calling but also as a strategic move to alleviate my college debt through loan forgiveness. My initial choice was the Navy, but when I went into their recruiting center, the recruiters were more interested in socializing with one another than attending to me. I did not have the time for this and walked a few blocks down to the Air Force recruiting center. Here I was warmly greeted and given all the information I needed to make an informed decision. Then and there, I decided to join the Air Force.

Before receiving my commission, I confronted a pivotal challenge—an essential state licensing exam. Our unique class, 1971A, stood as the first and only one to graduate in January. However, the New York licensing exam, occurring in July and December, necessitated a journey to Maryland in February. I was so fortunate that the Air Force recruiting team drove me from Brooklyn, New York to Baltimore, Maryland, where I joined classmates for a last-minute review, as we navigated the final hurdle.

In a surprising turn, the Air Force recruiters presented a proposition—providing my exam ID number would grant them early access to my results. I will never forget the morning when the phone rang. Answering the call, a voice on the other end asked, "May I speak to Lieutenant Batson?" and with those words, I learned that I passed the licensing exam! A wave of validation washed over me, and a sense of awe and wonder at the new life ahead of me.

I started on the next leg of my journey as I left the familiar streets of Brooklyn, New York, bound for Officer Orientation at Sheppard Air Force Base in Wichita Falls, Texas. Being commissioned as a 2nd Lieutenant thrilled my soul in ways I couldn't imagine—I was excited, amazed, proud, thankful.

Following the completion of orientation, I received my marching orders—to Wright Patterson Air Force Medical Center in Dayton, Ohio. Upon reporting to the Chief Nurse at the Medical Center,

I expressed a desire to be assigned to the Obstetrics/Gynecology ward since I had enjoyed working with moms and their newborns as a student nurse and had often worked with them as a LPN. However, I was informed that as a new graduate, I would need to spend a year honing my skills on a general medical floor.

Undeterred, I embraced the challenge, entering a realm where a diverse array of patients awaited care, each bearing unique diagnoses. The seasoned staff on the unit embraced me, their mentorship forming a nurturing cocoon as I navigated the nuances of patient care. The general medical floor became my training ground, a place where my skills sharpened, and my understanding of various medical conditions deepened.

The mentoring from the more experienced staff blossomed into a reciprocal exchange; I was a sponge, eager to absorb every ounce of nursing expertise, and they were eager to impart their wealth of knowledge. As I learned, the foundation of my military nursing career took root, nurtured by the wisdom of those who had walked the path before me.

As fate would have it, after four months of dedicated service, a window of opportunity swung open—a vacancy emerged in the OB/GYN unit, drawing me into the field of women's health. Stepping into this terrain, I found myself immersed in a world where compassion and expertise intersected, where every interaction held the potential to make a profound difference in the lives of those entrusted to my care.

Working hand in hand with the medical staff, I continued to embrace the role of a perpetual student, eager to glean insights and wisdom from seasoned practitioners. Even though many of these days were grueling with some impatient doctors, the love of what I was doing overshadowed the challenging days.

In the specialty of obstetrics and gynecology, I found my niche—a place where preparing women for surgery, tending to them postoperatively, and ushering new mothers through the sacred threshold of childbirth became my calling. Building rapport with patients became second nature, and as the days unfolded, I found myself listening to their stories, getting to know them, and anticipating their needs.

Beyond the confines of the hospital walls, I seized every opportunity the military offered for personal and professional growth. Engaging with various junior officers' groups, I embraced the spirit of camaraderie and the similar love many of us had to explore unknown places.

The allure of travel beckoned, and as I headed out on each adventure, I found myself enriched by the diversity of cultures and landscapes that unfolded before me.

One of my most memorable journeys was a pilgrimage to the enchanting land of Thailand with two nurse comrades. I was still dating the love of my life who asked me to marry him right before the trip!

I had told Cliff that I was going to be taking a hop to Thailand along with two girls and three guys. He promptly asked me out to dinner, after which we went to his home, and, in a private room of his house, he asked me if I would marry him. I said yes! I think he wanted to let the guys going on my upcoming trip know I was spoken for!

I proceeded on my trip and, dizzy with joy, boarded a cargo plane for Thailand. As we sat in the humble web seats, our nervous excitement mingled with anticipation for the awe-inspiring beauty that awaited us.

Nestled along the serene shores of Pattaya Beach, our house rental was a sanctuary amidst the magnificent expanse of nature's canvas. With each dawn, the sun painted the horizon with hues of gold, casting a spell of tranquility over the aqua waters.

As twilight descended, we took leisurely strolls along the shoreline, our footsteps leaving patterns in the sand until we discovered large pieces of driftwood to rest on. Here, we surrendered to the symphony of the waves, their melodic cadence a soothing balm to weary souls.

We ventured beyond the confines of our beachside retreat and found ourselves drawn to the vibrant pulse of life along the Chao Phraya River. In the early hours of the morning, we embarked on a boat on the waterway that served as a lifeline for countless natives, their lives intertwined with the ebb and flow of the river's currents.

The morning market unfolded before us, an array of colors and aromas, each stall a treasure trove of culinary delights and exotic wares. As we meandered through the bustling alleys, we were enveloped in the richness of local life, the air alive with the chatter of vendors and the laughter of children. With each passing moment, we immersed ourselves in the vibrant aspects of Thai culture, our senses awakened by the sights, sounds, and smells surrounding us.

Amidst the verdant landscapes and beautiful culture of Thailand, the rigors of travel faded into insignificance, eclipsed by the majesty of the journey itself. In those moments of wonder, I discovered that true adventure lies not only in the destinations we reach but also in the bonds forged and the memories etched along the way.

FLIGHT NURSE WINGS

Amidst the rigors of Active Duty, a new horizon presented itself—a coveted opportunity to attend Flight Nurse School, a six-week odyssey into the realm of Aerospace Medicine at Brooks Air Force Base in Texas. I gave my all during the course and I emerged adorned with Flight Nurse wings, a symbol of my enhanced proficiency in caring for patients during Medevac flights—an achievement that would shape the trajectory of my Air Force journey.

Yet, the Lord had more in store—an invitation to participate in groundbreaking research for NASA, a venture that would send me delving into the complexities of waste disposal systems in zero gravity. Alongside five fellow nurses, I embraced the thrilling experience of testing prototypes amidst the weightlessness of simulated space. At Zero Gravity, we floated about the aircraft like feathers. We could barely contain our excitement in our weightless state, and all six of us agreed there was no other feeling like it. The perks were plentiful—a respite from duty on Zero G flight days, a private tour of Houston Space Center, and an invitation to witness the historic Apollo night launch at Kennedy Space Center in Florida. It was spectacular!

The anticipation of witnessing history in the making infused the night with electric energy as we gathered beneath the stars, awaiting the spectacle that would unfold before our eyes. The roar of the engines, and the fiery trail of the rocket piercing the night sky—all bespoke of the ingenuity and spirit of exploration that defined the Apollo era. It was a once-in-a-lifetime experience. Our journey continued as we ventured into the heart of Houston, a city filled with life and energy. Tasked with the responsibility of transportation, I seized the reins of a station wagon, navigating the city's streets with a sense of purpose. In a culinary delight along the pier, I discovered the flavors of Houston's seafood—delectable tastes that lingered on the palate.

A hop to Spain became yet another chapter of exploration, as I found myself accompanied by two fellow nurses who were intrigued by tales of my previous adventures. In the vibrant streets of Madrid, we immersed ourselves in the rich Spanish culture, from the hallowed halls of the Prado Museum to the adrenaline-fueled spectacle of a bullfight. Evenings were adorned with the hues of theatrical productions, while the languid afternoons provided sanctuary for siestas, a cherished tradition woven into Spanish life. As the sun sank below the horizon, we indulged in the culinary delights of roast pig, savoring each morsel amidst the laughter and camaraderie that bound us together.

Yet, amidst the allure of travel, the promise of love and a future with Cliff beckoned me back to familiar shores. My fiancé's acceptance to medical school at the University of Buffalo, New York, marked a pivotal moment of decision, as I grappled with the realization that the confines of Air Force life could not accommodate our shared dreams. Dreams of having a family and a medical practice together. With a heavy heart and yet a sense of profound certainty, I tendered my request for release from active duty, a choice imbued with the promise of a new chapter unfolding.

As our wedding bells chimed in the bustling streets of Brooklyn, our life as a married couple began, full of sweetness and hope about the future that lay ahead. Amidst the misty splendor of Niagara Falls, we honeymooned, marked by whispers of romance and dreams yet to unfold. As we laid the foundation for our future in Buffalo, I found solace in the knowledge that no matter what marriage and family life required, the bonds of service and duty would forever tether me to the call of duty—I would be a reservist, ready to serve somehow.

I got a job at the Buffalo Veterans Hospital, which happened to be located across the street from the Medical School. We rented a three-bedroom duplex where our nextdoor neighbors were a young couple with triplet daughters. After one year, we were fortunate to purchase a home within walking distance to the VA Hospital and the Medical School. After both of us were comfortable, me with my work and he with the school, we jointly decided it was time to start a family.

THE BEGINNING OF MARRIED LIFE

With the arrival of our firstborn, Cliphane II, aka Cliff, we were amazed at how our hearts overflowed with love for our healthy baby boy. Yet, as the demands of parenthood beckoned, the rhythms of my job at the VA hospital shifted, casting a new light on my professional path.

In the late hours of the 3rd shift, amidst the hushed whispers of hospital corridors, I found myself immersed in the whirlwind of acute medical care. Though nights tended to be quiter, our patients still required around the clock care and us to be ready for an emergency at any moment. This late shift worked at first, as I could be with our son when Cliff was at his busiest with his studies.

I loved the camaraderie of my colleagues and the eager minds of medical students. Together, we navigated the complexities of patient care, each encounter a lesson in compassion and resilience. The bond forged between nurses and medical students was one of mutual respect and shared learning.

Yet, with the tender cries of our newborn echoing in my heart, I knew that the time had come to seek a new path—one less demanding and more conducive to the rhythms of family life. It was a bittersweet decision, tinged with the sadness of parting ways with colleagues who had become like family. We had shared the daily challenges of life, sensed each other's tensions, laughed at jokes shared; we had done life together. As I bid farewell to the medical students, I cherished the memories we had shared and the knowledge we had imparted to each other.

Though our paths diverged, the lessons learned and the friendships forged would forever remain etched as a part of my professional journey. As I embarked on a new chapter and the growing desire to be present as a mother, I carried with me the invaluable lessons learned in the halls of the VA hospital, forever grateful for the privilege of serving alongside such dedicated and compassionate souls.

I started working at the Millard Fillmore Suburban Hospital, another teaching institution which had the best equipment and staff and served a more professional population in the city. Here I resdiscovered my passion for the Labor and Delivery unit and found my love of women's health.

With each shift on the third floor, I found myself immersed in a world teeming with life and possibility, surrounded by the hum of new beginnings and the steady rhythm of labor pains. It was a place where new life unfolded with each breath, where the miracle of birth danced hand in hand with the art of healing. For me, Women's Health became not just a specialty—it was a calling, guided by the gentle hands of compassion and the unwavering commitment to the well-being of mothers and their precious newborns.

As a teaching hospital, it held a unique allure—a vibrant place of knowledge and discovery unfurling with each passing day. Here, amidst the eager minds of students and residents, I found myself rejuvenated by the spirit of collaboration and shared learning. But it was not just the thrill of academia that drew me to this work. It was the palpable sense of excitement that permeated the air, fueled by the presence of professional athletes and their expectant spouses. Their arrival brought a different kind of energy—an electric pulse of anticipation and celebration that electrified the atmosphere.

In the quiet hours of our home, I watched Doc toil tirelessly, his dedication to his studies unwavering despite the long hours and relentless demands of study. He stayed fueled by his unwavering commitment to his dream of becoming a physician. As the days stretched into weeks and months, I couldn't help but feel a sense of pride in his perseverance. And yet, amidst the chaos of his schedule, a glimmer of hope emerged—a possibility that would once again change the course of our lives.

The Air Force had a sponsorship program for medical students and I urged Doc to seize the opportunity, to dare to dream of a future where his aspirations could be realized without the burden of financial strain. With a heart full of hope and anticipation, he took the leap of faith and applied for the Health Professions Scholarship.

When the news came that he had been chosen as the recipient of the scholarship, our hearts swelled with gratitude and joy. As he stood before me, ready to take the solemn oath of office, I felt a sense of pride, knowing that I had played a small part in helping him achieve his dreams.

With trembling hands and hearts full of hope, as an officer, I administered the oath, each word a solemn vow to honor and uphold the principles of service and duty.

It was an honor to hear him say, "I, Cliphane McLeod, do solemnly swear that I will support and defend the Constitution of the United States against all enemies foreign and domestic…"

As the final chapter of medical school drew to a close, a new chapter awaited us on the horizon. With his diploma in hand and dreams soaring high, Doc started a one-year internship at a local hospital in Buffalo.

The next leg of his journey was a civilian residency in Obstetrics and Gynecology in the vibrant city of San Antonio, Texas. With eager hearts and a sense of anticipation, we said goodbye to the familiar comforts of home and set forth on the new odyssey, our belongings packed tightly into boxes as we prepared to write the next chapter of our story in the Lone Star State.

Amidst the bustling streets and sun-drenched landscapes of San Antonio, we found ourselves embraced by the warmth of a new community. And it was amidst the backdrop of this spirited city that we welcomed our second son, Lucien, into the world. With two small children and a need to work while Doc was doing his residency, I reached out to Ione, one of my cousins in Barbados. I offered her the opportunity to come to America to assist me with my two young boys so I could return to work.

Upon completing the required paperwork and jumping through the many bureaucratic hoops of the immigration system, her application for a visa was approved. We were overjoyed! She prepared to leave her siblings, and I prepared to receive her into our home. When she arrived, the boys seemed to be delighted to have another person in the house.

As we settled into our new home, I marveled at the experiences that awaited us, each moment a precious gift to be cherished and savored. San Antonio became not just a city, but a place to call home.

My first job in San Antonio was at Lutheran General Hospital in the Labor and Delivery and Newborn Nursery unit. The unit was short of staff and nurses were required to take calls. After having to repeatedly go to work in the wee hours of the morning I sought employment elsewhere. I returned to the VA Hospital system. This time, it was the Audie Murphy VA Hospital. I worked the day shift since there was a KinderCare center five minutes from my home where my older son, Cliphane now attended pre-K.

The hospital model of nursing was Primary Care. Each patient was assigned a nurse upon admission and that nurse cared for the patient on that and each subsequent admission. This time I worked in the Oncology unit. This model of nursing is extremely rewarding because you get to follow your patients throughout their treatment regimens. I quickly learned the different drug protocols. All of the experimental chemotherapy drugs were administered on my floor by PharmDs (Doctors of Pharmacy).

Besides working at Audie Murphy, I found a Reserve unit, the 32nd Aeromedical Evacuation Group, and was able to continue my reservist duty. Based on my prior experience I was tasked with the training of the medical personnel for fulfillment of the mission of Aeromedical Evacuation.

As we settled in, we had a joyful and unexpected surprise that would change life as it was. I discovered that I was pregnant—with twins! It was a revelation that filled our hearts with wonder and anticipation, a blessing that we welcomed with open arms and grateful hearts. And yet, amidst the joy of our growing family, the reality of our circumstances loomed large on the horizon. We had two sons, we were both working, and we knew something would need to change having to add two babies to the household!

With Doc's residency ending, the looming specter of his military obligation cast a shadow over our plans for the future. We knew we would be moving and with a sense of determination and resolve, we set our sights on a new horizon. Having spent those five long years weathering the icy embrace of Buffalo's winters, we knew we couldn't go back to that, and longed for a fresh start in a land where the sun kissed the earth with its golden rays. And so, with hopeful hearts, my husband submitted his request for assignment to bases in Arizona.

THE FAMILY GROWS

My prayers were heard, and we moved to the sun-drenched landscapes of Chandler, Arizona, where the sprawling expanse of Williams Air Force Base awaited our arrival—our next chapter. Leaving our home to the capable hands of a trusted realtor, we packed our belongings and our two young boys into our faithful Vanagon—a humble chariot that would carry us across the vast expanse of the American Southwest. As the sun beat down upon the open road, casting shimmering waves of heat across the desert landscape, we moved on.

With my swollen belly carrying the precious gift of twins, I reclined upon a twin mattress nestled snugly in the back of our minivan. The desert sun was unrelenting, its fiery embrace tempered only by the cool breath of the air conditioner unit that hummed softly beside me. With each passing mile, the landscape shifted and changed, a kaleidoscope of colors and textures unfurling before our eyes. Dusty plains gave way to rugged mountains, their jagged peaks reaching skyward in silent reverence to the majesty of nature's grand design.

Amidst the sweltering heat of a July afternoon, we pressed onward, our spirits buoyed by the promise of new beginnings and the thrill of adventure that beckoned us onward.

Shortly after we arrived, we discovered that one of my classmates from Flight School and his family with their two teenage sons were stationed there. They volunteered to have one of the boys drive me to the hospital if I went into labor while Doc was at work and of course, he happened to be at work when I went into labor!

When I was admitted to the hospital it was discovered that the second twin was breech. I had a skilled obstetrician who was Doc's partner, and since Doc was the new obstetrician on base and we were having twins, there were about ten people in the delivery room. The nurse could only hear one heartbeat, so I had to have an ultrasound followed by pelvimetry (measurements to see if I could deliver vaginally). They found that one baby was in the breech position. By the time the testing was done, I was ready to deliver! I was fortunate that I was allowed to have a vaginal delivery.

The first twin, Travis, was my largest baby and weighed seven pounds. The doctor tried to turn the second baby around but was not successful so he felt for the feet, which he had Doc hold while he reached for the body and delivered him through a breech extraction. Fortunately for me, Nicel was only five pounds and nine ounces. My entire labor and delivery was two and a half hours, too short for worry!

On the evening of my delivery, I experienced severe itching on my abdomen, and I developed a rash that started on my abdomen and spread to my entire body. The medication given was ineffective and the rash soon turned into purple splotches. There was no dermatologist on staff at our hospital, so I had to be sent to Luke Air Force Base a little more than an hour away to be evaluated and diagnosed. My workup consisted of many tests including for autoimmune disease, all of which were negative, thank God. After a few days, I was discharged home with my baby boys and my body rash.

I never received a definitive diagnosis; it was thought to be idiopathic (cause unknown), and the rash lasted seven weeks. Whenever I went out people would stare at my purple splotches. I was given Benadryl for the itching of the rash and developed severe high blood pressure. I could feel my temples pounding and prayed that I would not have a stroke and be unable to care for my newborn babies. It took several weeks for the blood pressure to return to normal.

Following an otherwise normal postpartum course, I resumed my Air Force Reserve duty, this time at Luke Air Force with the 41st Medical Services Evacuation Squadron. Life was busy and it seemed the children grew in leaps and bounds.

I was the training officer for the 41st MSES (Medical Services Evacuation Squadron) and was, amidst other things, tasked with traveling to Osan Air Base, South Korea, to make arrangements for our unit to participate in the '89 Team Spirit exercises. The hospital facility had to be inspected; housing accommodations had to be made; and supplies had to be inspected as well.

Thankfully my cousin still lived with us, so I didn't have to worry very much about disrupting the children's routines. The twins were seven and a half years old when I went to South Korea and then returned back there three months later with our team for an eleven-day military exercise. Here, we participated in the multi-service exercise with the objective of testing and evaluating the operational readiness of the contingency hospital facility, the Aeromedical Staging Facility (ASF), the Blood Transshipment Center along with the other support systems, such as Central Supply and Pharmacy.

Participation in Team Spirit '89 provided an excellent learning experience for all members. It is the participation in such exercises that highlights why monthly training is an absolute necessity for Aeromedical Evacuation Squadrons who can be called into active service at any time with only a few hours notice.

The 41st Medical Services Evacuation Squadron Unit was tasked with covering the Medical Evacuations Service out of Hickam, Air Force Base, Hawaii once a quarter. I had the privilege of being the coordinator on several occasions. Hawaii is a place that I was paid to go to, and I used my free time there to enjoy the gifts of the Creator—the ocean, mountains, vegetation, and the sunshine.

I had decided that our four boys would be the extent of my family, but as the saying goes, "God's plans are not our own." I became pregnant in 1984 for the fourth time and delivered a beautiful, healthy baby girl, Natacha.

Upon completion of his tour of duty in Arizona, Doc decided that a military career was not what he wanted, and so the search for a different opportunity began, and it led him to an area I had never considered living. He accepted a position at a 30-bed hospital in Hinesville, Georgia. We found a house that was under construction and, with the assistance of the hospital, purchased it. We returned to Arizona to put our house on the market, pack up, and prepare to move. My precious cousin, who had become an integral part of our family, had met the love of her life and decided to remain in Arizona. A new journey, literally and figuratively, laid ahead.

GEORGIA LIVING

On this trip, I was able to help Doc with the driving. With five children in tow and changing drivers, we took our time, made several stops, and three days after leaving Arizona, arrived in Hinesville, Georgia.

Office space was at a premium in the area near the hospital, so Doc rented a house which he turned into his practice. The office was five minutes from the hospital. If there was a patient about to deliver, he could go across the street to the hospital, do the delivery, and return to continue seeing his office patients. Since Doc was the only practicing obstetrician in the area, his practice grew rapidly.

I volunteered in the office while the children were in school. The practice quickly outgrew the initial office space, so we moved into a larger office space. It was also a house which we had converted into an office. The practice was now large enough that I worked as a nurse and became the business manager. I conducted classes for the staff, purchased supplies, consulted with company representatives about necessary models of office equipment, and provided the necessary documents for the accountant so that the needed income taxes and Workmen's Compensation payments could be prepared.

The local hospital was limited to routine normal deliveries. Some procedures required the patient to be admitted to a Savannah hospital, which was about an hour away. Doc obtained temporary privileges there and was able to do surgery and also consultations for other doctors at that hospital.

On several occasions, the office experienced leaks from heavy rains, which damaged some charts. The landlord attempted unsuccessfully to fix the leaks. It was at this time that I encouraged my husband to think about building his own office, especially since there was no material advantage to continue paying rent, and there would be significant tax advantages from doing so. Initially, he hesitated because we had built a house a few years earlier, and it was a huge undertaking. After giving it much thought he agreed, and we were able to find a lot for sale with excellent highway access for his patients. It was less than fifteen minutes from the hospital, which was convenient should he have to do a delivery during office hours.

I met with the architect and gave him a schematic of what was needed for the office building. I thought that if we had two suites, one for the doctor, and the other for rent, we could easily pay the mortgage. Upon completion of the building, a dentist, who was separating from the Army, offered to lease the suite. Sometime after we moved into our building, the local hospital decided that it would no longer offer obstetrical services, so Doc, as he became known to all by then, had to decide what to do about the hundreds of patients he was serving.

As he had been granted limited privileges at a hospital in Savannah and had done surgeries and consultations for other doctors before the hospital decision, he spoke with the administrator of the Savannah hospital and was granted full privileges. This meant that his patients would now have to travel for at least 45 minutes to deliver their babies. Some of these patients had no means of transportation, so arrangements had to be made in advance for them to get to the hospital.

I continued working in the office on a part-time basis so that I could be available for the children's extracurricular activities. The children were doing well in private school, Doc had a thriving OB/GYN practice, and we had built our dream home. I had never imagined that this kind of life would have been possible for us in the South. I only expected to find a place to raise my children comfortably away from the rat race of big city life.

THE CHILDREN

All five of the children were involved in athletics, and we spent many hours traveling to and from those activities. The boys primarily played soccer and baseball. The two eldest, Cliphane and Lucien, also played basketball. Natacha played soccer and tee ball.

We eventually purchased a recreational vehicle, and I was able to carry several of my children's teammates when we traveled out of town or out of state for games and tournaments. On one such occasion, while traveling to a soccer game in Atlanta in a convoy, one of the vehicles needed gas, so we stopped at a BP gas station in Griffin.

One of the players from another vehicle came to me to get some Tylenol for his headache. As a nurse, I always carried medical supplies with us. While I was giving the player Tylenol, one of my twins decided to go into the store to buy some Pringles potato chips. Unaware that he was not in the motorhome, I continued on to the sports complex in Atlanta. We arrived, and the players left the motorhome and went to the field to warm up. My twins had accompanied me but did not have a game that day, and some of the siblings of other players had come along with us. During the game, I saw some of the children playing on a grassy slope, which appeared to be covered in something resembling poison ivy. I yelled at them to come down, which they did, except there was only one of my twins, Travis. I asked him to get his brother, and he said Nicel was not with them.

So, the search began. Some of the parents who were in our convoy assisted me. We searched the adjacent neighborhood park with children who were playing and inquired if anyone had seen my son. Upon questioning those who rode with me, one boy said that the last time he saw him was in the store at the gas station! My heart sank. The BP gas station was more than an hour away. Fortunately, there was a police substation on the grounds of the complex, and I asked for a phone book and looked up the phone number for the gas station, asking the receptionist to dial the number for me, so that I could speak to the attendant. She did, and the attendant told me that after my son had been standing by the door waiting for me for quite some time, she approached him and asked him to come inside with her.

He told her that his mother said that if they were ever separated, he should not leave, and she would always come back and get him. It had been quite some time since she first noticed him, so she called the local sheriff, who she knew had young children himself. He came and took Nicel along with his kids for a burger. Nicel was a true soul. He told the attendant at the gas station that his dad was working and gave her his dad's beeper number, (this was before the advent of cell phones), so Doc was aware of our son's whereabouts before I was. I felt even more awful because it was our anniversary weekend, and I was out of town with the children and I had lost his son.

When I told the coach what had happened, he hurried the players into his van, and we must've driven 90 miles an hour to get back to the gas station to recover my lost boy. Nicel was ashamed because he did not tell me he was leaving the motorhome. The other children in the motorhome were playing games and watching TV and had not noticed that he had not returned. I was so happy that he was safe that I was not angry; I was more concerned about what his dad would have to say when we got home. We were grateful that his guardian angel never left his side. My apprehension about Doc's reaction was unnecessary because he, too, was happy that his boy was safely back with us. Nicel has written so many papers throughout his middle school, high school, and even college years about what happened the day he went to a BP gas station in Griffin, Georgia to buy Pringles. Needless to say, from that day on I kept a notebook with the names of all the children who rode with me and did a roll call before and after each stop we made.

TEAM SPIRIT '89, OFF TO WAR

I was unable to find any unit vacancies for me to continue my reserve duty in Georgia so I commuted to Arizona for monthly drills. One of my assignments there was to participate in Team Spirit '89, which was a multi-service exercise in South Korea. In the fall of 1988, I was asked to go to South Korea to plan for the accommodations and training for the members of our unit who would be participating in Team Spirit.

The exercise provided outstanding training, not only for our unit but was pivotal in testing the operational readiness of the contingency hospital and its support services. Several days after our unit arrived, we were augmented by the 21st Medical Evacuation Squadron of Florida. I met the commander of that unit who later told me that he had a vacancy in his unit for a training officer, especially one with my experience in readiness preparation. This ended my monthly commute to Arizona and marked the beginning of what would become some of the most fulfilling, yet frightening, times of my military career.

It started with the unit Commander's call in January 1991. This meeting usually took place at the end of the weekend drill; however, on this day, it was held right before lunch. The Commander identified 25 members who should meet with him at the end of the day. It was at that meeting that our unit was notified that we had been activated and were being deployed to a secret destination. We were to be prepared to report to duty within 24 hours of being called. I was filled with apprehension because Saddam Hussein had invaded Kuwait. Our unit's mission was to operate a field hospital, and I thought that was where I might be going.

I was scared, and Doc was angry! He had told me a few years earlier that I should get out of the military, but I had not taken his advice. He reinforced to me that I had *volunteered* for this assignment.

My five children were now 15, and 12, the twins were 9, and 6. The children attended private school, and although my oldest son had a driver's permit, he was not yet licensed to drive. I made transportation arrangements for them to get to school, which was on two different campuses in the city. Many questions raced through my mind. Had I made all the necessary arrangements for the care of my children? Would my husband be stressed by their many activities?

My cousin, Ione, had once told me that if I were ever deployed, she would care for the children in my absence. One call to her was all it took. She said yes, I purchased her ticket, and she was on her way from Arizona to Georgia. I knew that the children would be well cared for.

Two days after that Commander's call, the dreaded notification came. The following morning, I sent my children off to school, said goodbye to my husband, and went off to war! I checked into my unit, got the required immunizations, filled out the necessary paperwork, got last-minute necessities and a few hours of sleep.

Early the following morning, I boarded a military aircraft along with the other members of the group, and we flew into Dover Air Force Base in Delaware on that cold January morning to await our military transportation to Saudi Arabia. My sister drove from New Jersey to meet me there and went to the chapel to pray for my safety and the safety of our group. As we prepared to board our flight, I was told that I was the senior officer on the aircraft, and, as such, was appointed Troop Commander, which meant that I was responsible for ensuring that all of the troops on the manifest boarded the plane and reached their stated destination. When we arrived at Dhahran Airport, the group from my unit boarded a bus for our destination Al Jubail.

It was during that long flight that I had a heart-to-heart with the Almighty. I recall asking Him to protect me and return me safely to my children. I asked God not to allow my children to become orphans, like me and my sister. A calm soon came over me as I remembered Isaiah 41:10, "Do not fear, for I am with you, I am your God, and I will strengthen you, I will help you." I am positive that quiet reassurance carried me through the turmoil of the deployment.

The bus dropped us off in the middle of the desert. There were several pallets with equipment at our location. As we wondered where our direction would come from, an officer from another location came and gave us directions about what was expected. We rolled our sleeves up and pitched the tents that would be our home for the duration of the war. We spent several hours filling sandbags to fortify our tents.

The day after we, 21 MSES, arrived, we were augmented by 96 members from Scott Air Force

Base, Illinois. This group included three flight surgeons, nurses, technicians, and also some administration staff. A few introductions were made, but there was a lot of whining. "What are we supposed to do out here? Where are our quarters? Where are the showers?" The new arrivals soon joined us, and we quickly set up tents for the additional members.

The British troops who had arrived sometime before us were an amazing resource for us. One of the flight surgeons from Scott AFB was appointed Commander of the entire group, and I was appointed Assistant Commander. I selected one of the nurses from the Scott contingent to be the Chief Nurse, and we began to erect what would become the Aeromedical Staging Facility (ASF), or what is more commonly known as the MASH unit. Part of our day was also spent on constructing a bunker, which was also fortified with sandbags. We filled thousands of sandbags. Fortunately, being in the desert, our material was right there at our feet.

At 0315 the morning, after we completed the building of the bunker, we received a SCUD missile alert. We donned our gas masks and headed for the bunker. This was to be the first of many such alerts. During the day we trained for the mission, which was to care for wounded soldiers, while they awaited flights for definitive care at major medical facilities. We were told to expect hundreds of casualties. Thank God that did not materialize.

We trained 12 hours on and 12 hours off to be ready for the anticipated wounded. Our days were extremely busy. Not only was I the Assistant Commander, who had to oversee all the training, but I was also appointed the mayor of our compound, which housed the Air Force, Navy, and Marines. Being mayor meant that any issues within the compound that affected our readiness or negatively impacted the troops were brought to me for resolution.

In less than five days, our ASF was fully operational, and the American flag was raised for the first time. While we waited for the arrival of casualties, we continued our training. The Commander, who was a flight surgeon, decided that while we were waiting for patients he would log in some flying hours on one of the planes that visited our compound that was flying to Germany. Unfortunately for him, he got snowed in just as the ground war was getting underway.

The unit from Scott AFB was quite concerned that several days had passed and there was no word from him. Central Command was notified. Following many days of absence and no communications, Central Command appointed me Commander of the 5th TAC ASF, as we were then called. Thus followed a flurry of meetings to notify all units in the vicinity of the change of command. This included the Marines, the Navy, and the British, all of whom were located in the area.

Exactly one month after arriving in Saudi, my life changed drastically. My base unit only made up twenty-five percent of the troops. Just imagine the chatter when I announced that we would be having a Commander's call at a time when there was no word from the Commander. It was at that meeting that I informed the troops that I'd been appointed the new Commander of our unit. There were many questions along with lots more chatter. Why? Where was Dr. P? Why had we not heard from him?

The troops knew I had extensive experience with training, having been the Officer in Charge of training for three different units and during a joint service exercise, but could I lead a multi-service unit during wartime? After all, the medical officers in the unit were all men, and I was a black female. I am sure there were questions about my leadership capability. The members of the 52nd from Scott felt the leader from their unit had abandoned them.

It was during this time that I leaned heavily on prayer, which has always been my go-to, and every time there was a chaplain in the area who would say "mass" I would attend. I found this to be the source that provided the confidence that I needed to carry out my new role. I had the support of Central Command and my home unit from the beginning. Judging from how well the units coalesced to complete the mission successfully, my leadership was no longer in question.

I led admirably under the most difficult situation: wartime, in the most austere location: the desert. I give praise to my heavenly Father for His guidance and protection, leaning on Psalm 28:7, "The Lord is my strength and my shield: my heart trusts in Him, and I am helped; therefore my heart greatly rejoices, And with my song I will praise Him," (NKJV). I am thankful He granted me the wisdom needed to lead well during the deployment.

Our ASF was the busiest one during the ground war. Our facility received 452 admissions, and most of them were Marines, followed by the Navy. We were the only site where Air Force and Navy medics worked together. Some of the personnel in the unit were teenagers who had never left their home state, and they were petrified, working under wartime conditions. I had frequent Commander's calls to remind everyone of the mission and to praise them for their performance in these challenging surroundings. The morale remained high, and we continued to train 12 hours a day.

Each night I took whatever moments I could for prayers, and my heart and thoughts would drift to my family at home. To stay connected and let the children know I loved them, I wrote several letters each week to them. I had a few occasions to go to Bahrain and could call home from there, as there was no way to call in the middle of the desert. It warmed my heart to hear all was well at home for those brief moments. I wiped a tear from my eyes and entrusted each of them to my Heavenly Father to watch over them. Then I hurried back to the desert and the busy days waiting for me.

The air war only lasted 17 hours. The war was over, but the ASF had to remain open to care for any casualties who needed to be flown out, so we remained in readiness mode and prepared for our redeployment. Inventory had to be taken, sandbags had to be emptied in areas that were consolidated in anticipation of our redeployment.

As we prepared to dismantle what had been our living quarters for two months, I felt that since we were in the desert and used very little of our allotted budget, I would reward these amazing troops with spending the last night not in tents but at a hotel.

The Holiday Inn at Al Jubail was the most ornately decorated hotel that I had ever seen. There were marble floors throughout and exquisite chandeliers on every floor.

On our long journey home, we were treated like royalty. We were sad to be separated from our new "family" but happy to leave the miles of desert, the sand, and the SCUD missile alerts behind. On the final leg of our flight, one of the flight attendants on American Airlines had recently celebrated her 25th anniversary with the airline, and as a sign of gratitude for our service, gave me the pin that the airline had given her for her service. It was such an honor for me made even more meaningful because I lived in Georgia and had to reunite with my family and could not participate in the Florida victory celebrations for my base unit. I could not go off again and leave the family. I can only imagine how afraid they must have been seeing the news coverage of war and knowing that I was in the midst of it.

I was overjoyed once arriving home to hug my children and spend time with them exploring their feelings about me being at war. They all said they understood the call to duty, and it helped them get through the weeks without me. They were afraid for me and so happy when their dad said I called. I smiled as the twins eagerly let me know that a local TV station had visited the school interviewing them because their mom was deployed.

Another wonderful aspect of being home was being able to sleep in a bed. After sleeping on a cot for almost three months, any bed was pure bliss!

PARENTS MOVE TO GEORGIA

Life soon returned to normal, as if I had never left, yet in the serene streets of Hinesville, Georgia, a notion stirred within Doc and I—a desire to provide warmth and comfort for his aging parents now in their late seventies. They were weary of the chill and burden of snow-laden winters in New York.

Doc was the firstborn of their two sons and our children were their only grandchildren. We broached the subject delicately, extending an invitation for them to join us in the embrace of Southern hospitality.

Their worries, etched upon furrowed brows, melted away at the prospect of escaping the harsh grip of northern winters. They also had an understanding of our family responsibilities and gladly felt it was their duty to participate and be there for the children. Longing for closeness, they embraced the idea of moving to Coastal Georgia.

In a stroke of serendipity, a house materialized just a stone's throw away from our own, so with eager anticipation my in-laws embarked on a journey of relocation, leaving behind the icy tendrils of winter for the gentle caress of Georgia's warmth.

For my children, the arrival of Grandma and Pops heralded a new chapter of joy and connection. The children were most proud when they would attend their sporting events or Grandparents Day at school. Pops had been a chef at the Waldorf-Astoria Hotel in New York for many years and was an excellent cook. Both my in-laws were from Jamaica, West Indies, and prepared many meals in their native cuisine, which besides being tasty were an educational experience for the children.

With each passing day, they all reveled in the simple pleasures of daily visits, but not long after Grandma and Pops arrived, my father-in-law's battle with diabetes cast a shadow upon our lives. He had the big toe on his left foot amputated, but it would not heal. His surgeon then used a conservative approach in an attempt to save as much of his foot as possible by doing a trans-metatarsal amputation (removal of the remaining toes). This procedure was also unsuccessful, so finally, after trying many kinds of treatments, he had a below-the-knee amputation followed by hyperbaric oxygen treatments, which aided in the healing process.

During this time, he also required many trips to Savannah, an hour away, for follow-up appointments with his doctors. Since I worked part-time in Doc's office, I was available to take him to his treatments and appointments.

He was eventually fitted with a prosthesis and resumed driving locally with trips to the bank and supermarket. I was not only his daughter-in-law but also his caretaker, and he asked me if I would take him to an attorney so that he could write a will. When I brought him, he gave me Power of Attorney over his affairs.

None of these repeated surgeries and challenges seemed to get him down. Amid the trials and tribulations, his resilience shone like a beacon, guiding us through the darkest nights. With unwavering determination, he faced each hurdle head-on, his spirit unyielding in the face of adversity.

Meanwhile, my mother-in-law began having some cognitive issues, so she needed to be assisted with tasks such as personal care, writing checks, and shopping. I was now responsible for seeing that my in-laws had what they needed for day-to-day functioning, and the nature of Doc's practice was such that his availability, unfortunately, could not be counted on.

On top of caring for my in-laws, my children were in four different schools, and I was the one who provided their transportation. At the end of some days, with each task performed, each errand run, exhausted to the bone, I drew strength from the words of Galatians 6:9, "Let us not grow weary of doing good, for in due season we will reap a harvest if we do not give up." This was a beacon of hope amidst the weariness of the journey and kept me going.

Without warning, Liberty Memorial Hospital in Hinesville decided to discontinue providing obstetrical services and Doc had to decide whether to stay in Georgia or leave the area. He had developed a relationship with Sister Mary Faith, the hospital administrator, who offered him full privileges upon the condition that he relocated closer to St Joseph's Hospital in Savannah for liability reasons. Our home in Hinesville was an hour from the hospital without traffic. We had a decision to make!

As we looked at the options before us, we found a lot for sale in Richmond Hill, which is about halfway between his office in Hinesville and the hospital. We purchased it and built our dream home there. After we built our house and moved to Richmond Hill, it became evident that having my husband's parents forty-five minutes away was not ideal. We asked them if they would be willing to move closer to us and, by divine providence, a house came on the market diagonally across the street from us. It felt like a hug from my Heavenly Father; a sweet reminder of Proverbs 3:5-6, "Trust in the Lord with all your heart and lean not on your own understanding."

AN UNFORGETTABLE BIRTHDAY

Amidst the hum of office routines and the ebb and flow of daily tasks, Wednesdays held a special rhythm—a collaboration between the Nurse Midwife and me. While she tended to the needs of patients, I assumed the mantle of business manager, orchestrating the administrative duties that kept our practice running smoothly.

My responsibilities included ordering supplies, balancing accounts, and ensuring our team remained abreast of regulatory requirements. Each task was an integral part of the system, woven with care and dedication to our shared vision of providing exceptional care to our patients.

Yet, amidst the familiar cadence of office life, a discordant note pierced the air—an unexpected summons to Doc's office, where reprimand awaited. Despite having followed protocol and seeking authorization for a schedule change for the midwife, notifying the office manager to schedule patients accordingly, our actions were met with disapproval, leaving us bewildered and disheartened. As we retreated from the confines of his office, I attempted to lighten the mood with a jest, a feeble attempt to dispel the tension that lingered in the air. Jokingly, I said to the midwife, "We just got our hands slapped."

Walking down the hall I turned around to see Doc standing in the doorway to his office. I don't know if he heard me. It was my birthday that day, and the office celebrated birthdays with a potluck, a birthday cake, and ice cream so we did what was customary.

With the echoes of celebration still ringing in my ears, at home after dinner that evening I was called into the study where Doc said, "Joan, I don't want you back in my office, and I don't want you to touch the checkbook!" The revelation came like a bolt from the blue. Baffled and bewildered, I sought answers. "Can you tell me what this is all about? What have I done?" He would not say. He just said, "If you don't like it, you can get yourself a divorce lawyer!" I was devastated! My pleas for explanation were met with cold silence and the threat of dissolution looming ominously on the horizon.

Not only was I the business manager, but I had also been an office nurse who was dedicated to making his practice one of the best in the area. I thought maybe he would reconsider. I was numb. For about a month, I pondered my next steps and prayed for guidance.

In the wake of this seismic shift, I grappled with the weight of betrayal and uncertainty, my sense of identity shaken to its core. In that moment, I realized that loyalty and dedication were but fragile threads in the tapestry of relationships, easily frayed by the capricious winds of change. And as I stood at the crossroads of despair, I wondered if redemption and reconciliation would ever find their way back to me. I wasn't sure who I was without my work at the office. My spirit was crushed by Doc's rejection of my work . . . of me. I had given my all to him and to the business I thought was ours. It was as if I floated in a surreal vacuum.

I had to ask for money to manage the household, and I was told I should get a job. I had not worked in a hospital setting for almost two decades. Despair knocked at my door, but being resilient, one who always pushes through with dignity, I straightened my shoulders, grit my teeth, and dug deep. Since my last work experience was in Labor and Delivery, I decided to apply for a position as a Birth Assistant at the Birthing Center. With trepidation and a hint of nostalgia, I ventured back into the realm of employment, seeking solace and purpose amidst the corridors of the Birthing Center.

The delivery experience at a Birthing Center is unique in many aspects. Laboring women can have something to eat up until the time that they are ready to deliver and are free to walk in the center or even outdoors since they are not tied to the bed with intravenous fluids running. There is even the opportunity to have a water birth. Some women choose to deliver their babies in the water of a specially designed bathtub. Within 24 hours of delivery, the woman can go home.

I was filled with joy at the prospect of assisting women through labor and delivery again. Gone would be the days of managing household and practice finances, replaced by the sweet anticipation of guiding expectant mothers through the transformative journey of childbirth.

As one who not only survives but chooses to thrive despite circumstances, I clung to this experience before me as I buried the pain of change. I believed and knew that "God works everything for good for those who love Him and are called according to His purpose," (Romans 8:28). If the requirement was to simply love God, I had that in abundance.

After a successful interview and tour of the Center, I was told that my hiring would be dependent on having passed the Neonatal Resuscitation certification. When I inquired about the dates that the local hospitals gave the certification class, I was encouraged to apply for a position in Women's Health at the hospital. I was not sure I was ready for that kind of a schedule.

At the encouragement of my friend and fellow nurse, Beth, I reluctantly completed the application. Soon thereafter, Beth told me that she had spoken to the Coordinator of Women's Health about me and said the Coordinator wanted to speak with me. I had an interview with Wendy, after which, she called Human Resources to tell them that she had spoken with me and that I could fill a vacancy. Off I went to HR and after another interview, I was hired on the spot to work on the Mother-Baby unit. I worked full-time at the hospital, choosing the night shift to avoid being in my husband's way, and I worked part-time at the Birthing Center.

In the familiarity of the hospital's bustling corridors, I found a renewed sense of purpose and fulfillment, each day unfolding like a precious gift waiting to be unwrapped. As I stood at the helm of the newborn nursery, guiding both new mothers and eager nursing staff alike, I felt the warmth of contentment wash over me like a gentle tide.

With each tender moment shared with new mothers, I witnessed the blossoming of confidence and mastery, their eyes alight with the joy of newfound knowledge. It was a privilege to be a part of their journey and to stand witness to the miracle of motherhood unfolding before my eyes.

The offer to lead the newborn nursery on the second shift came as both a surprise and an honor, a testament to the trust placed in me by my colleagues and superiors.

As I immersed myself in the intricacies of newborn care, I found myself guided once again by the timeless wisdom of Proverbs 3:5-6, "Trust in the Lord with all your heart, and lean not on your own understanding; In all your ways acknowledge Him, and He shall direct your paths."

This divine guidance illuminated my path with each step forward. And amidst the whirlwind of responsibilities, I found unexpected blessings, from social security contributions to the promise of a future retirement plan.

Little did I know then the profound impact that my time in the hospital would have on my future—shaping not only my career but also my financial security. In the tapestry of life, each thread woven with care and purpose, I found myself grateful for the unforeseen blessings that bloomed amidst the challenges of the journey.

I continued working at the hospital for nine years, and Doc kept working at the practice. Only by God's grace could I walk down the path of staying in my marriage. I was upset at the way I had been treated, yet not being one for conflict, I avoided it at every turn. The atmosphere in the home was cold, and Doc and I maintained distance from each other—intimacy feeling like it was a lifetime ago.

The children knew that their father and I had grown apart from one another. They were all away at college by then, and when they came home to visit, we were all cordial toward each other.

RETIREMENT

In 2010, I started a home-based business working with new technology in the television and telephone business. I found joy in the new people I met in this network marketing world. It was a fun investment and way ahead of its time—selling a phone that you could dial anywhere in the world and see the person you connected with. In February 2013, after experiencing persistent leg and foot pain, I decided to retire from full-time nursing and give more time to my business. I attended international events in many different cities and even received recognition at several meetings for being in the customer club.

It was at one such meeting that I called Doc to let him know I had arrived safely. He told me he had slept in the recliner because he had so much pain in his leg he could not walk to the bed. He asked our son who lived nearby to get him an anti-inflammatory, which he did. Getting no relief several hours later he directed our son to call an ambulance to take him to the hospital the following day.

I arrived back in Atlanta and my daughter drove me straight to the hospital in Savannah. Because Doc's chief complaint was pain in his leg, the doctors initially felt that he had thrombophlebitis (inflammation of a vein), so he was treated for it while they waited for his lab results. His lab work showed that he was having an acute attack of gout.

It was determined that since this diagnosis was now different from his admitting diagnosis, he should be discharged with medication for gout. His very astute nurse, realizing that he had not been out of bed during his stay, notified the doctor caring for him. Fortunately for my husband, he was not discharged, because a few hours after his proposed discharge he suffered a stroke. The stroke was mild, but this meant that he would have to go through the hospital's rehabilitation program.

During this hospital stay, Doc informed me that he had filed for bankruptcy and that we would have to vacate our home of twenty-two years. While he was in rehab, I would have to look for a house to rent, pack up our belongings, and get them moved. He told me we had to leave the house in thirty days. I was blindsided and overwhelmed. I became furious.

I tried retracing the steps that had led us to this point of financial ruin. Sometime before this all happened, I recalled him saying we were going to refinance the mortgage as another bank had taken over the mortgage and raised the interest rate. I thought it made sense. The agent came to the house for us to sign the paperwork and said that I should have the new mortgage in his name alone and I agreed. I always considered the good of others before my own. Then this happened! My anger increased!

As I tried to make sense of this timeline of devastation, I remembered that day in 2003 that Doc told me in no uncertain terms that I was not to work in his office. I pressed him for reasons for my dismissal, but he declined to give me a response.

I had worked so hard, and the patients loved me and the extra time I spent caring for and educating them about themselves and the babies they were carrying. They knew they could count on me to assist them with breastfeeding if the need arose, as it sometimes did. I was doing payroll, keeping office staff updated on the state regulations and the many changes occurring in the healthcare field, and also purchasing office supplies. Along with all of those responsibilities, I also paid the office bills. Doc had a thriving practice.

He had two offices in different cities and operated on a schedule of three days in the main office and two days in the other. It would have been impossible for him to oversee and accomplish everything I did. He did not hire anyone to replace me. No wonder there was such chaos!

I was beside myself but heard my inner voice repeating the words of Paul in Romans 12:17, "Bless and do not curse, take no vengeance, vengeance is Mine, saith the Lord," (KJV). Yet I had to allow the thoughts and feelings to flow through me—all of this was the result of him firing me. He could not keep up with the financial side of the business and run the practice as well. He tried but did not listen to the signals from his body and ended up with a stroke!

I forgave him because I knew that having ill will against anyone only hurts you and not the person you have bad feelings against. He was the love of my life and the father of my children. I had to set an example for them, not merely about commitment, but of God's grace to each of us when we make a mess.

So I set out trying to find us a house while he lay in his hospital bed. There he had plenty of time to think about the ways he had managed the gifts God had given to him. God would say to him what needed to be heard.

I eventually found a house to lease. The lease was for one year since the owner was a contractor working overseas and would be returning stateside in a year. We were approved for the lease based on my credit information. Doc earned a lot of money but neglected to pay his bills on time and now also had bankruptcy on his record so he had poor credit.

I hired a moving company to move the large items with the intent of having my sons come into town to help with the smaller items. The children could not believe what had happened. In disbelief and kindness to me, none of them expressed their feelings to me other than to let me know they would be around to help me with moving. We made many trips between the two houses. Needless to say, after twenty-two years we had accumulated lots of stuff. When the deacon from my church learned of my situation, he and his wife came to help me pack up some things and brought their trailer, loaded it up, and moved the things to the rental house. I will be eternally grateful to Deacon Doug and his wife Renee for their kindness.

A deep sadness enveloped our every step. We had that mansion built, and I had spent countless hours picking out wallpaper, colors for carpet, tile for the kitchen floor, light fixtures—all my heart ever dreamed of. How could he do this? Tears of frustration, anger, sadness, and grief flowed at losing it all. And—he had bought a boat for $125K! Meanwhile, Doc continued his rehabilitation. How I needed God and pressed deeply into Him.

On one occasion, when I went to pick up items from the home, I discovered that the power had been disconnected for nonpayment. Since we were no longer living there Doc did not want to pay to have it reconnected. In despair and fatigue, we simply left many treasured things behind at that house. Things I would choose to not even think about later so as not to conjure up an even deeper sense of loss.

When Doc was discharged from the hospital, he had in-home physical and occupational therapy and was soon able to return to work. Since his stroke was mild, he had no residual effects, but he had to walk with a cane due to a previous injury in his right hip from a motorcycle accident.

He was pleased with the home that I had selected. There was adequate room for the children when they visited for holidays and special events. The owner of the home flew in and did a mid-year inspection and asked us if we wanted to extend the lease for another year. We happily agreed, but shortly thereafter, the Army changed the owner's contract, and we had to move out. Once again, I began my search for a house to buy. For me, it was not acceptable to continue renting houses.

THE UNRAVELING

The home search was exhausting. I combed through listings and toured countless properties; my heart yearned for a place where cherished memories could be made—a sanctuary where we all could feel at home.

And then, after looking at several houses in the Stonebridge community in Savannah, I stumbled upon it—the perfect house, nestled serenely with woods on two sides. It was a beautiful, eleven-year-old, single-family home with a formal dining room and a spacious kitchen with gorgeous granite countertops. The oversized master bedroom had an en suite bathroom with a separate shower. Upstairs there was a bonus room, which added to the five bedrooms and three-and-a-half bathrooms, with one of the largest lots in the community located at the end of a cul-de-sac. This would become my new home, with ample space to accommodate the laughter and joy of my children, grandchildren, and the generations to come; it was a place to flourish.

Now retired with a fixed income, having already downsized, I stood on the threshold of this newfound treasure, not sure how I could pay for it. A familiar face emerged as my steadfast ally—my oldest son, Cliphane, whose unwavering support and generosity helped me with my down payment. The path to home ownership became a shared adventure. I was able to close and move into my very own home three months shy of my seventieth birthday. God is SO good! The hand of God has been on my shoulder throughout my life. There are many times when I could have let doubt and even despair overtake me, but I have trusted in Him and He has never let me down.

Just when I thought that I was settled in my new home and routine, along came a sense of vuja de. It was September 2016. I had planned to travel to Monroe, GA to celebrate my Cliphane's birthday and that of his twin daughters, who just happened to be born on his birthday. Doc was to come up after he finished at the clinic on that Friday. I called to see if he would be on his way soon, and he mentioned he had an episode of chest discomfort during the night but stated that it must have been due to the pizza sub that he had eaten for dinner. I told him that he should have that checked out, and he said that if it recurred he would. I mentioned it to the children, and they were concerned and called him and asked him to please have himself checked to make sure it was only indigestion before he got on the highway for four hours.

He reluctantly agreed to see his primary care doctor as soon as he finished with his clinic, who agreed to see him right away. His doctor did an electrocardiogram and sent him straight to the hospital where he was admitted. He was having an impending heart attack. Cardiac catheterization determined that he would need open heart surgery. Incidentally, the dye used for the catheterization knocked out what kidney function remained after thirty years of diabetes.

Doc wanted a specific cardiac surgeon to perform his operation, but he was not on call. He asked that the surgeon be notified so that he could prepare to do his surgery the following Monday. The doctor who was covering told him that as long as his condition remained stable, he would wait until Monday.

Meanwhile, Doc insisted that we stay and celebrate the birthdays since there was nothing that we could do until after the surgery. We celebrated the birthdays, and on Sunday morning the children and I came home to be with him the night before his surgery. The open-heart surgery went well but the recovery was long and difficult. After thirty-four days in the hospital, he was discharged with in-home physical and occupational therapy.

As a nurse, I have always found males to be more difficult patients than females, and my physician husband was no exception. He was often noncompliant with the directions from his therapists.

After a few weeks with little or no progress, I felt that he would benefit from daily therapy at a rehab facility, but initially, he refused. The in-home therapists urged him that he should consider inpatient therapy which was daily and would be more beneficial. He was interviewed for admission, and it was at this time that the coordinator from the facility informed me that he had not completed the hospital's rehab program so his insurance would not cover additional inpatient rehab. He had told the hospital staff that his wife was a nurse, and she could assist him with his rehab! His only recourse now was outpatient rehab.

I obtained the necessary referrals, and he was admitted to outpatient rehab. Three days a week I loaded up the wheelchair and off we went to rehab and on the alternate days he had to go for dialysis.

I would drive him to dialysis, go home, and after three hours I would pick him up. His dialysis lasted four hours.

At outpatient rehab, we met a male therapist from Scotland who was instrumental in Doc's return to full ambulation. It took six months before he was fully ambulatory with the use of a walker. Needless to say, he was forced to close his clinics. Two employees were kept on staff to provide patients with their medical records and to offer them referrals to other providers.

The practice had never upgraded to digital records and had every paper chart for the thirty years of his practice. The records that did not need to be kept had to be broken down and separated so that they could be shredded.

My cousin, who was an employee, and Nicel, my youngest son, who had decided to move home from Orlando, were such a great help with this monumental task. What an undertaking this was, there were two offices and thousands of records to be disposed of. Many hours over several months were spent in this endeavor.

Doc showed no interest in anything that had to do with the office. Understandably so, his practice had become his life, and now, that part of it was over. However, this left me with the arduous and overwhelming task of having to close his two office locations in two different cities.

I say this not to complain about how much had to be done, but to point out that I was fired by the good doctor. "The stone which the builder rejected has become the cornerstone," Psalm 118:22 (NKJ).

During this process, I prayed for patience and perseverance.

One day, I mentioned to a colleague that I needed to find a local company to shred charts, and she told me to check with her secretary, who gave me the contact information for someone locally who was willing to be of service. What if I hadn't asked? As it was, it took many months of working several times a week to get rid of the outdated charts. How long would this have taken without the help?! The office could not be rented with all the medical equipment, furniture and charts left behind and all would have been delayed further. I was so thankful God impressed me to get help.

While waiting for Doc to decide about the disposition of the office, not one but *two* inquiries were made about purchasing our office building. After some negotiation, an agreement was reached for the sale of the building, which by this time had been vacant for two years. The oral surgeon, a tenant for thirteen years who rented the adjacent suite for his practice, decided that he should own the building.

It was early summer 2021 when Doc noticed a large blister on the big toe of his left foot. He had been wearing sandals and did not know how it happened. His foot doctor opened and dressed it and gave him a follow-up appointment.

Upon his return to his doctor, there was no noticeable healing, and the toe could not be saved, so he was scheduled for a procedure to assess the circulation to his foot. It was determined that because of his diabetes, the circulation to his lower extremity was not good and that a blood vessel graft was needed to improve the circulation so that the incision could heal once the amputation of the toe was done.

The bypass graft was done and after the surgery, he was told it was a "Hail Mary graft" since he had so few vessels that could be used. The graft worked well, and the left big toe was subsequently amputated. He was given a boot and taught the correct way to ambulate in physical therapy to compensate for the missing toe. His post-surgical appointments found the graft functional, and the incision healed without any problems. After an uneventful postoperative course, he was able to drive himself to dialysis three times a week.

Doc became interested in flying drones, and this became his retirement hobby. He took a course in the intricacies of the sport and eventually became licensed. On any day the weather permitted, he would travel to different locations and fly his drones. During this time, we were also able to attend some Atlanta Braves baseball games in Atlanta as a family event with the children.

One afternoon in late January of 2023, Doc asked me to look at the second toe on his right foot and, lo and behold, it had a large blister. I asked him to make an appointment to see his foot doctor as soon as possible, which he did reluctantly. It was decided to watch the toe and measure the progress toward healing. Unfortunately, there was no progress and soon the adjacent big toe also developed a blister, while the second toe started to become gangrenous.

This was not the outcome that was hoped for, and the decision was made to do another graft—this time on the right leg. Doc was admitted to the hospital for the graft. Unfortunately, this time he had no vessels of his own for the graft and it was decided to do a cadaver graft. The graft was then checked frequently to determine if it was functioning. Meanwhile, the blister on the big toe got bigger and there was no evidence of improved circulation to the second toe. After a few days with no evidence that this graft was functioning, the second toe on the right foot was amputated. After a few days in the hospital, he was transferred to Encompass, a rehabilitation facility. By this time Doc was not walking and he needed physical therapy in order to resume his pre-surgical activity.

He became depressed and would eat only if being fed. Two of my sons and I took turns making sure that we were there at mealtime to supervise and assist him with his meals. It was during one such occasion that he turned to me and said, "You are a good wife." I thanked him for the compliment. It was not often that I heard him express gratitude in this form. He had said in the past that I was a good mother, nurse, nurturer, but this was the first time he ever said to me that I was a good wife. I received it as a kindness to my soul that somehow brought peace, affirmation, and healing. Did I need him to say this? No, I did not. Was it good to hear him say it? Yes, it was.

About ten days into his rehab, he decided that he wanted to be discharged, although it was recommended that he continue his therapy. His doctor reluctantly discharged him. Four days later at his post-operative visit, his surgeon determined that the cadaver graft was not working; the surgical site was not healing and his vital signs revealed that he might be septic. The hospital was called and at the time of the call there were no beds available, but several discharges were pending so we were told to go home and wait for a call.

The call came many hours later. He was admitted and scheduled for a below-the-knee amputation. The surgery was done the following morning. After a few days of observation, he was discharged back to the rehab hospital.

His depression was now more pronounced. I urged him to eat so he could regain his strength and go home, and his response was that he was "damaged goods" and didn't want to be a burden. My response was to remind him that his father was in his eighties when his diabetes course followed the same path, and he healed, got a prosthesis, and resumed his activities of daily living, which included driving to the bank and the grocery store. "Pops had the will to do it," he said.

A few days postoperatively, the surgeon was changing the dressing and decided that he needed to take Doc to the OR to clean up the surgical site.

When they opened the site it was infected and the doctor notified us that an above-the-knee amputation was necessary to save him from sepsis. The operation went well, but because he was already septic, his vital signs remained dangerously low and he could not have the breathing tube removed. He was taken to the ICU. He remained on the ventilator but regained consciousness. Since his vital signs were quite low, he could not receive dialysis, which by this time he had now missed several times due to his surgery and unstable postoperative course.

On his third postoperative day, since he appeared to be breathing well, he was weaned from the ventilator for several periods and tolerated it well, so he was taken off the ventilator. On day four it was decided to give him nutrition by mouth. He started the normal progression from clear liquids, which he tolerated. In the evening, when his meal came, he seemed to be pleased with the full liquid diet. I fed him the cream soup, the vanilla custard, which he enjoyed, and some of the protein shake.

Our daughter, Natacha, had driven from Atlanta and one of our sons was visiting so we turned the television on, and we all talked about the upcoming Braves game. Visiting hours were over for that time so I came home and prepared our dinner. Natacha returned for the final hour of visitation, and she watched the Braves play with Doc until it was time for her to leave. He told her to be safe going home. At about 6 am the following morning, we received a call from the hospital stating that Doc was experiencing respiratory problems and that we should come in. Natacha and I notified our two sons who were living in Atlanta and then headed to the hospital ourselves.

Apparently, an hour earlier he told the nurse he was having problems breathing, and they had to re-intubate him. He had been on massive doses of antibiotics for the sepsis and medication to bring his blood pressure up—all to no avail.

He did not appear to be conscious, but we talked to him letting him know that we were there with him. The doctors all came and explained that he had been through so much in a short while that his body was giving out and so we prepared to say our goodbyes. After a couple of hours, it became evident that his body had shut down. No matter how much medication he received his vital signs never improved.

We awaited our last son's arrival, and then, he was pronounced.

In the quiet stillness of the hospital room, surrounded by the gentle hum of machines and the soft glow of fluorescent lights, the once-vibrant physician lay at rest, his journey through life's tumultuous seas finally drawing to a close. For thirty long years, he had walked the halls of medicine. In the bustling towns of Hinesville and Savannah, his hands had worked miracles, bringing new life into the world with each gentle touch and each whispered word of encouragement. Thousands of babies had felt the tender embrace of his care, their first cries echoing through the corridors of the maternity ward like sweet melodies of hope and promise.

And yet, amidst the joy of new beginnings, there had also been moments of sorrow and pain. Hundreds of women had entrusted him with their lives, allowing him to wield his scalpel with skill and precision, knowing that in his hands, they were safe. And though his patients had come from far and wide, drawn by the promise of his expertise and the warmth of his compassion, it was here, in the heart of the coastal plains, that his legacy would forever be etched into the fabric of time.

As he lay there, surrounded by the gentle embrace of loved ones and the quiet dignity of his final hours, he found peace—a peace that transcended the confines of earthly suffering and the relentless march of time. For in the stillness of that moment, he was free—free from the burdens of the world, free from the relentless march of medical machines that had been his constant companions in his final years. My deep sadness was coupled with relief as I knew he wouldn't have wanted to live as an above-the-knee amputee. He would have needed to be taken to dialysis three days a week and be totally dependent on me for his care. He was once a vibrant man who was proud of his many accomplishments who now felt that he was no longer a whole individual.

And though his journey had come to an end, his spirit lived on. For in the hearts of those he had touched as a doctor, his memory would forever burn bright, a guiding light to all who dared to walk in his footsteps and carry on his legacy of healing and hope.

A NEW BEGINNING

In the quiet moments of reflection, I found myself unraveling the threads of my journey—the joys, the sorrows, the triumphs, and the trials that had woven together to form the intricate story of my existence.

For amidst the countless new beginnings that had punctuated the chapters of my life, there existed a quiet resilience—a steadfast resolve that had carried me through the darkest of nights and the fiercest of storms. And as you, dear reader, have journeyed alongside me through the pages of this story, perhaps you have found yourself wondering how I could remain so steadfast, so unwavering in my positivity.

The truth, as always, is multifaceted—a tapestry woven from the threads of love, faith, and the indomitable human spirit. It is the love of family and friends, whose constant support has been a beacon of light in the darkest of times. It is my faith that has sustained me—a steadfast belief in the power of hope, of resilience, and of the inherent goodness that resides within every one of us. The story of the power of God that sustains and gives life.

It is the resolute conviction that every new beginning, every twist and turn of life is an opportunity for growth, learning, and transformation. For in the crucible of life's challenges, we are forged anew—stronger, wiser, and more resilient than before.

As I look at my life, I do so with a heart full of gratitude and a soul ablaze with the light of possibility. Woven into the fiber of my existence, I have found not just the threads of hardship and adversity, but also those of hope, joy, and boundless possibility. And it is in the weaving together of these threads that the true beauty of life is revealed—a tapestry rich in color, texture, and meaning, waiting to be unfurled with each new dawn.

As a teenager, I remember standing amidst the gentle rustle of palm trees hearing the soothing melody of waves lapping against the shore. The sun dipping low on the horizon, casting a warm, golden glow over the tranquil shores of Barbados.

It was here that I came to understand the true reason behind my father's decision to bring me to live with my grandmother, the story of my mother not being able to endure the woes of what she endured at his hand.

As I gazed out at the endless expanse of turquoise waters stretching before me, I made a solemn vow to myself. I promised myself that I would never allow myself to be diminished by anyone, especially not by those of the opposite sex.

From that moment onward, I became a beacon of strength and independence—a force to be reckoned with, unyielding in my determination to carve out my own path in this world. With each passing day, I embraced the challenges that lay before me, drawing strength from the lush beauty of the island that had become my sanctuary.

And as the years unfolded, I remained true to my promise, standing tall and unwavering in the face of adversity. For I knew that no matter what obstacles may come my way, I possessed the inner strength and resilience to overcome them—to forge my own destiny and to chart my own course through the ever-changing currents of life.

So as I stood there on the shores of Barbados, surrounded by the timeless beauty of nature's bounty, I knew that I was more than just a survivor—I was a warrior, a fierce and indomitable spirit, unbound by the limitations imposed by others. And at that moment, amidst the whispers of the wind and the gentle caress of the sea, I found solace in the knowledge that I was truly free—to be exactly who I was meant to be, without apology or compromise.

This was, oddly enough, one of the reasons Doc was attracted to me! So, in May 1973 when I stood at the altar of St Barbara's Church in the presence of God, before the priest and a church of witnesses, I entered into a covenant that had as an obligation to stand by my partner in good times and bad, for richer or poorer, in sickness and in health 'till death us do part. God has promised us blessings in keeping this covenant. Mark 10:8-9 tells us that what God has joined together, let no man separate.

We were a couple for fifty-five years. It was not always easy, but it was worth it. Out of our relationship came five amazing children, and Doc's parents enjoyed a quality life in their declining years because of it.

I was never afraid of being alone or of not having money. As a nurse, I could make enough money to take care of myself, and I knew that I could rely on the promise that God would provide.

Often, we get caught up in what we want and do not consider the good of the unit as a whole. Yes, I supported my husband throughout medical school, internship, and residency and would have loved to become a Nurse Practitioner, but was it worth breaking up the family unit? My doing this would have prevented me being flexible for my family and our already compact lives. I say no! Raising my family, supporting our household, was a priority for me. With prayer for guidance, I channeled my energy into being the very best Registered Nurse that I could be at the time.

I have always found strength in attending Mass and Holy Communion and I know this practice helped me through the ups and downs in my marriage. I was constantly being reminded of God's promise to be with me always no matter what I was facing. He is faithful to His promises. We must place our trust in Him and He will see us through whatever we may be struggling with.

I now find myself traversing the winding paths of life as a widow—a journey marked by both sorrow and resilience yet illuminated by the radiant love of family and the quiet whispers of purpose.

Each day unfolds with a delicate dance of support and companionship, as I pour my heart into nurturing my children and grandchildren, reveling in the simple joys of their laughter and the warmth of their embrace.

Amidst the ebb and flow of life, my home-based business has evolved, with new and varied products that speak to the essence of creativity and innovation. Though my involvement may be limited, there remains a sense of fulfillment in the rhythm of sorting through junk mail, tending to my garden, and embracing the serenity of stillness of daily living. I do have commitments that have their own routine meetings and responsibilities and keep me connected to communities that have been part of my life. I am on the Board of Trustees at Savannah Christian Preparatory School, a Lector and a Minister of the Eucharist and past President of Parish Council at St Stephen Catholic Church in Hinesville, where I have been a member for thirty-seven years.

As I pause to reflect upon life, I am filled with a profound sense of awe and gratitude for all that I have accomplished. For despite the trials and tribulations, I have navigated life's tumultuous waters with grace and resilience, guided by the unwavering compass of fulfillment and purpose.

In these quiet moments of reflection, I am reminded that true happiness, contentment, and fulfillment are not found in the external trappings of success, but rather in the depths of the human spirit. It is a journey of self-discovery, rooted in the core strength bestowed upon us by the divine—a reminder of who we are meant to be, and the boundless capacity to love that resides within us all. In this realization, I find solace and peace, knowing that I have lived a life rich in love, purpose, and meaning, guided always by the gentle hand of God.

ABOUT THE AUTHOR

Joan McLeod retired as a Lieutenant Colonel from the United States Air Force and made her home in Savannah, Georgia along with her youngest son, Nicel, and Harley, her Newfoundland. Joan loves to travel and has completed medical mission trips to Nigeria and Haiti.

She is a group leader for Non-denominational Women's Christian Conferences. She enjoys gardening and is a source of encouragement through inspirational text messages she shares daily with her network of family and friends.

MARIGOLD PRESS BOOKS

Relationship focused, independent publisher sharing stories of hope.

Marigold Press Books was created to build a legacy by sharing stories of hope and magnifying the voices of women. Founders Emra Smith and Rebekah McLeod saw a gap in the industry that left budding authors wandering and aimless. Their intention is to provide a relationship focused publishing experience where they guide authors through the entire process from idea inception to published book to marketing and more.

Visit Us
www.marigoldpressbooks.org

Instagram
@marigoldpressbooks

Email
marigoldpressbooks@gmail.com

www.ingramcontent.com/pod-product-compliance
Lightning Source LLC
Chambersburg PA
CBHW070146080526
44586CB00015B/1870